Real Leaders Give a Damn

RESTORING HUMANITY TO CREATE WINNING TEAMS

Cory Galbraith

Copyright © 2019 Cory Galbraith

All rights reserved.

ISBN: 9781082792151

DEDICATION

This book is dedicated to you, the reader, who cared enough to acquire this book. It tells me that you "give a damn" and for that, you are to be congratulated.

CONTENTS

Acknowledgments

1	Introduction	Pg 1
2	That Confusing Word "Leader"	Pg 4
3	Remembering John – A Real Leader	Pg 6
4	Will Caring Create Profit?	Pg 11
5	The Cost of Not Caring	Pg 13
6	Get Real	Pg 16
7	Pay Attention to What Your People Want to Talk About	Pg 19
8	The Fine Art of Listening	Pg 21
9	Creating Tomorrow's Leaders	Pg 25
10	Putting the Meaning Back into Work	Pg 29
11	Even After They Leave	Pg 32
12	Being a Real Leader is Risky, but it Shouldn't be	Pg 35
	Epilogue: In Defense of Managers	Pg 37

ACKNOWLEDGMENTS

I need to acknowledge the 250,000 people from all over the globe who took the time to read and comment on my original social media article about John, the Caring Leader from which this book is based. You provided the inspiration I needed and, in that regard, you are all "real leaders." I also thank my friend and colleague
Stefan Zaichkowski, whose advice and unwavering belief in me, allowed me to realize that maybe, I do have something to say after all.
For the incredible people on my team, and in my family, I'd be nothing without you. Finally, a shout-out to John, who through some social media digging, has been discovered, happily still communicating with all the people he has helped over the decades.

1 INTRODUCTION

I often test the content of my books on social media first, to find out if there is sufficient interest out there. When I did that for this book, I was both shocked and saddened. I also felt overwhelmed by the sheer volume of comments from people who said they had never experienced a caring leader.

Not ever.

One reader wrote that in 22 years of working, he hadn't met a manager who took the time to truly listen to him. Another talked about a supervisor who saved the life of a co-worker having a heart attack, only to be fired for taking the time off to help save a life.

Many people told stories of neglect, like the millennial hired for her first job, given a desk and simply told to "get to it." No training, no orientation. Not even a simple "welcome".

I heard about how hard-working people are being abused every day - through indifference, bullying and a total disregard for the basic human need to feel validated.

Even people in positions of authority expressed disappointment at upper management who they said viewed anyone at the "bottom" including, and especially "middle management," to be easily replaceable because "there are more waiting in line."

There's a lot of pain. More than I anticipated in the course of my writing and research.

Admittedly, I also heard from people who did work for caring leaders. I was fascinated to discover that these people remembered their leaders for many years. While they may have worked for amazing bosses only a short time, the influence of these caring leaders lasted a lifetime. Those who cared long ago passed the torch and gave birth to new caring leaders.

In producing a book about caring leaders, one should expect to be criticized. There is still a strong view out there that any kind of caring is a sign of weakness, to be avoided at all cost. I heard from one manager who referred to his employees as "losers" who didn't deserve his time because the only thing that was important is profit.

So how did we get to this place? How is it possible, with the avalanche of material on good management and leadership, and with an explosion of communications technologies, supposedly designed to bring people closer to understanding – to still have what is arguably the largest leadership vacuum in history?

For the most part, I will leave it to the psychologists to answer that question. But there is little doubt in my mind that today's levels of stress, our obsession with "self" and the compulsion to demonize people who might look, speak and think differently from us - all has something to do with it.

The state of the world, the rise of fear, the dizzying pace of, and obsession with, technology, and an uncertain future, it would seem, have conspired to turn leaders into tyrants. Otherwise "nice" people simply don't have the time to care. At least not in a sincere way. It's been beaten out of them. The worry about their own status under corporate "re-organization" and the pressure to produce better profits from the last quarter take precedence above all else.

And yet - we see strong evidence that the caring for our people, and the long-term sustainability of our companies, churches, governments and organizations - are intrinsically linked. When employees are treated well, they, in turn, treat customers well.

This is not a traditional management book or guide to leadership in the conventional sense. There is enough of that out there already.

This is really a book about how to restore our humanity. How to be kinder to each other. How "caring" can put back the meaning so many of us desperately seek.

Within these pages, I believe, is an urgent message that needs to be heard, loud and clear, in boardrooms everywhere: A real leader gives a damn about people.

A business, or any organization for that matter, is based upon its people. If the leader cares little or nothing of his or her people, what does that say about the leader's commitment to the organization? Are they not one in the same?

You don't need a title. And you don't need years of experience. But you do need a heart.

On a personal note, I must make one confession. There was a time, years ago, when I was the opposite of what this book is advocating. I was an uncaring leader. Like many new managers, I excelled as a technician - knowing exactly how to do the work - but I was horrible at dealing with people.

I yelled at my team. I impatiently looked at my watch as they poured their hearts out to me. I told them if they didn't like working here, I could show them the door.

I didn't care. And they knew it.

Perhaps this book is my way of saying sorry, to make amends, but mostly, to help turn the tide.

Because if you're running an organization, a department, a team - or any kind of group, including a family, even if it's just you and one other person - you have an enormous responsibility to build people up, not tear them down.

You're in a unique position to help reverse the widespread culture of neglect.

We need you, desperately, to be a real leader.

2 THAT CONFUSING WORD "LEADER"

**"A leader is best when people barely know he exists, when his work is done, his aim fulfilled, they will say: we did it ourselves."
- Lao Tzu**

Reaction to this book, when first released, was mixed. And it began with the title.

Firstly, in some cultures, the word "damn" which means "damnation" is used only in the negative context, as in "I don't give a damn." The title, therefore, caused a bit of confusion with some people believing that I was saying that a real leader is someone who *doesn't* care.

It's generally accepted now, in North America at least, that "damn" can also be used in a positive context. The word has some punch, so I opted to go with it for the title. I could have just as easily used the title "A Real Leader is Someone Who Cares." (I use the terms "real leader" and "caring leader" interchangeably throughout the book).

Now to the word "leader".

Has there ever been a word so misunderstood?

The official definition of a leader is someone who "leads or commands a group, organization, or country."

But many people today assume that a leader is a boss, manager or supervisor, anyone with a title denoting some level of authority. A boss is defined as someone in charge of another person, or an organization. But does being in charge mean they're also looking out for that person's best interests?

And a manager is someone responsible for "controlling or

administering all or part of a company or similar organization." That might mean overseeing paperwork and have little to do with people.

I found the official definitions to be a bit confusing so I checked the meaning of the word "lead" and found explanations like these: "An example for others to follow" "Holding others by the hand to move forward" "A position of advantage as in taking the lead".

It would seem, therefore, that a leader is different from a boss or manager. A leader is someone who "shows the way" and in most of the recent literature, is considered to be a person who inspires others. A boss or manager may not necessarily do that, although they can certainly be leaders too. Someone who is not a boss or manager, but is a front-line worker, could also be a leader, if they are inspiring and guiding others, despite the fact they have no title.

In the military, a "leader" is viewed as someone who has the power to save lives. He or she provides the direction to accomplish a mission of combat and puts the needs of the troops and the country ahead of their own personal needs. Military leadership can be seen as completely selfless. We often hear the term "of service" (service leadership) when talking about people in the military.

How many business leaders would put the lives of their teams ahead of their own? Actually, some would - and have (as has been the case with workplace shootings in the United States).

If a leader is someone who is "leading" then it would seem obvious that they care about the people they're leading - or at least, should. Why then do I use the term "real leader" (as in "caring" leader)?

I did so deliberately because of all the confusion that exists out there.

The word "real" is meant to emphasize the point of this book - that we need to care about the people who work for us and with us.

That's real.

Food for thought: Are you just a boss or a leader?

3 REMEMBERING JOHN – A REAL LEADER

"The task of the leader is to get their people from where they are to where they have not been." - Henry Kissinger

The following article was written by me for social media and struck a nerve with many people. For days, in response to the article, hard-working people from around the globe acknowledged, by name, the bosses who cared about them the most and made a lasting impact on their lives. What was fascinating about this reaction was that people were "giving a damn" about their managers. The opposite of my main message. But caring is reciprocal. If we care about our people, we not only inspire them to grow, both as professionals and as self-sufficient human beings, we also experience the added benefit of feeling good about making this a better planet.

In this short article, I remember "John," a manager I had worked for whose impact on my life, I am sure, is far beyond what he could have ever imagined. It's been 30 years since I worked for John, but that's how long a caring leader can influence you.

To me, John embodied everything a real leader who cares is all about. I therefore decided the best way to begin the book was to tell his story.

A Real Leader Gives a Damn About You Even if You Leave

He was my boss years ago who left a lasting impression on me for one reason: he gave a damn.

In fact, John cared more about me and my career than he did about the needs of the company, at least, that's the way he made it seem.

How about you? Can you remember a favorite boss? Why do you remember them? It was likely because they cared too.

They cared about you, your career, and your future. They wanted the best for you, even if it meant you had to leave and go in a different direction.

Today's fast paced environment leaves little time for caring. That's why the caring boss is rare, and the most valued kind of leader.

People will work hard for someone who cares about them.

The caring leader is special in 10 ways.

1. The caring leader shows a sincere interest in the welfare of his or her people. They take the time to ask about our health, our dreams, our concerns, our family and our goals – and, they actually listen to the answers.

2. The caring leader is there for the long term. Rather than being resentful, the caring leader will congratulate departing employees, wish them the best and make themselves available as a mentor if and when needed. Even though you leave the organization, the caring leader may still be there for you, in touch long after you leave.

3. The caring leader provides the tools for success. Caring leaders arrange for training, support and encouragement, knowing that as we get better, so too will the organization.

4. The caring leader practices honesty. Caring leaders won't lie to us. They will tell the truth and commit to do their best in serving us and the organization.

5. The caring leader takes the time to listen. They won't write off our concerns as trivial. While they may not always be able to help us, they will at least hear us out and empathize.

6. The caring leader follows through on promises made. The best bosses I have had did what they said they were going to do, and if circumstances made that impossible, they would explain why and how to keep going at the earliest opportunity until success was achieved.

7. The caring leader points out our talents and positive traits. They want to build on our strengths, more than change our weaknesses, knowing that exploitation of strength is the fastest route to success.

8. The caring leader cheers for us. They genuinely want us to succeed.

9. The caring leader arranges help when needed. Rather than quickly dismiss people experiencing depression, grief or life trauma, the caring leader will arrange appropriate help to see us through, so we can emerge as positive, strong contributors.

10. The caring leader is sincere. People can spot a fake in a second. Pretending to care won't cut it and will backfire, every time.

Back to John, my former boss for a minute.
Never before, and not since, have I witnessed a more caring manager.
Like all department heads at one time or another, he had to let go of some people. But all the people he ever dismissed maintained a very high regard for him. That's because even after letting them go, he would stay in touch and see how he could help them.
In some cases, if a person acquired special skills he later needed, he would re-hire that person. In many cases, he helped people get other jobs, more suited to their skill set.
I don't know where John is today, but I know one thing – his caring, remembered to this day, created incredible loyalty and dedication. In the end, it was not only we who served under him who gained, but the entire organization was the better for it.

It's not about title. It's not about seniority. It's not about being a "boss". It's about giving a damn.

End of article

Of the people who reacted to this article, many had their own definition of who a real leader is, based on their own experiences. Here's what they said, in no particular order. A real leader is someone who…

- gives a damn, otherwise, they're just a manager
- gives a damn, even if nobody else does
- supports you even when you fail
- leads by example
- doesn't leave you hanging
- has your back
- fights for you
- stays hopeful, even in bad times
- practices empathy
- serves his or her people
- admits when they made a mistake
- creates other leaders
- leads people to success
- grows talent, and is not a roadblock to growth
- shows pride in their people
- has a sense of humor
- does not micromanage
- is transparent with no hidden agendas
- practices good self-leadership
- gives honest feedback
- checks to see if you're okay
- isn't afraid to lead by example and get their hands dirty
- isn't afraid to show their humanity
- doesn't berate people publicly
- others want to follow, not because they have to, but because they want to
- puts the needs of the team ahead of their own

And that's just a short list. Clearly, this is a topic people care about passionately. Readers reminded me that people don't leave companies, they leave managers and that my article explained that. The frustration out there with managers who don't give a damn is enormous, and, it is sad. Because as human beings, I believe we all have it in us to be caring.

Food for thought: Are you like John?

4 WILL CARING CREATE PROFIT?

"Everyone talks about building a relationship with your customer. I think you build one with your employees first."
- U.S. business executive Angela Ahrendts

There are caring leaders but also caring organizations. These companies and groups are generating healthy profits more and more as caring becomes a powerful differentiating factor within a competitive landscape of greed, cut-throat tactics and relentless marketing.

People magazine publishes a list of companies that care the most, according to their readers.

Topping the list are software firms such as Intuit and Adobe, and accounting/financial giants like Deloitte and Edward Jones - not necessarily the type of organizations you would think are in the caring business.

But senior management at these progressive organizations believes in paying attention to what employees need and want. In many cases, employees are eager to increase the meaning of their contributions - if not through the tasks they're paid for, then at least via volunteer work. As a result, you'll find programs that pay employees to take time off so they can help their favorite causes.

Ultimate Software has developed a transgender workshop open to all employees with the intent of creating a safe, inclusive environment.

File hosting service Dropbox has a unique program to improve the wellness of employees, providing $100 towards sports equipment so employees can reduce their stress levels.

All of these firms have a healthy bottom-line.

But the question begs to be asked - can caring turn around a company, from near bankruptcy to becoming top in its field?

It certainly did at the Ford Motor Company which was facing extinction in 2006 until a boss named Alan Mulally came along. (The year 2006 was one of the worst years ever for Ford when it lost close to $13 billion).

At the heart of Mullaly's strategy to make Ford a winner again was the cultivation of mutual respect. The company created "best teams" where people committed to excellence were band together and told they could not operate out of self-interest. Instead - managers, team leaders and every line worker - had to challenge each other to do their best. In effect, "care" for each other. The "best teams" were comprised of people who gave each other credit whenever solutions were found (rather than competing with each other to take the credit).

Respect was a big issue for Mulally. Managers had to buy into what was referred to as Ford's "culture of consideration."

And it wasn't just employees who got treated like human beings. Ford's car dealership owners did too. Mulally actually once had his employees at a corporate meeting look the dealers in the eye and tell them that they were loved.

In a world where caring is in short supply, it sticks out whenever it appears. Employees notice, but so do customers, especially millennials who will make up 75 per cent of the workforce by 2025 as baby boomers pack it in and retire.

According to a 2016 study by Come Communications, 64 per cent of millennials won't work for uncaring companies that are not socially responsible.

There can be no doubt about it. Caring leadership is good for business.

Food for thought: Caring is a competitive advantage.

5 THE COST OF NOT CARING

"Toxic people attach themselves like cinder blocks tied to your ankles, and then invite you for a swim in their poisoned waters."
— John Mark Green, Author of "Taste the Wild Wonder"

There is a high price to pay for not caring in today's workplace. It's a price being paid every day not only by the people who work for us, but our organizations and society as a whole. As managers we're paying a price too – in tarnished reputations and a deterioration of our own self-esteem.

Ignoring people, treating them "like dirt" (in the words of many who reached out to me in the course of my research) and putting them at the bottom of the priority list are resulting in immeasurable emotional pain and suffering, lost productivity and burgeoning health care costs. The culture of neglect is doing something else too: it's contributing to our collective sense of defeat, giving us little to look forward to.

If your leadership refuses to uplift people, then let it at least not hurt them.

A recent Gallup survey found that almost half of all workers in the United States report feeling burned out at least some of the time. That burnout, according to a report by CNBC, is resulting in $200 billion in health-care spending every year, much of it to combat heart disease and high cholesterol.

A lack of caring has something to do with it.

The consulting firm "Life Meets Work" conducted a groundbreaking leadership study finding that 56 per cent of employees feel they're in a toxic workplace, one in which subordinates are often publicly belittled.

Another study, by Everest College, revealed that 75 per cent of American workers view their immediate boss as being the most stressful part of their work day.

Researchers for the American Psychological Association say that people's need for acceptance and purpose is not being met at work. To quote an Association report: "Bad managers criticize and ostracize their employees, micromanage and strip them of autonomy and support, and behave erratically, keeping their employees in a constant state of stress."

The culture of neglect and abuse is not just dominating the American landscape. It's everywhere.

In Japan, work is literally killing people. In fact, it's happening so often that the Japanese have invented a word for "death by work" called *karoshi*. USA Today reports that many Japanese in their 20s are working much longer than the average workaholic in North America, clocking up to 160 hours a week (which leaves just 8 hours to sleep over the course of 7 days).

Japan is relentless in its pursuit of economic growth. And people are paying with their lives. The country's culture of overwork has led to countless suicides and severe illness causing death.

Unfortunately, and this is the part you may not like or agree with, but much of the research puts the blame on managers, many of whom are woefully unqualified to lead.

A good number of managers are promoted because they are high achievers for the company. But their success at selling or getting things done does not necessarily translate into people skills. In fact, such a transfer is all too rare.

If you, as the boss, decided to be more caring towards your team, would each team member bounce into perfect health? Would they be happier? More productive? Would you be doing society a favor?

There are no guarantees, and everyone is different, so the question is complex. But in the larger scheme of things, considering the overwhelming evidence – the answer has to be yes.

But what if you, as a manager, are a genius at managing tasks and budgets – but possess not an ounce of empathy for people – perhaps not even towards your friends and family? The question I pose to the executive boardroom is – should you be a leader of people at all?

Perhaps only those who care should be in that position.

Food for thought: Think of the damage you're doing by withholding a caring attitude.

6 GET REAL

"Leadership and learning are indispensable to each other."
-John F. Kennedy

After I published my article about John, the Caring Leader, a good number of people remarked that they were working for bosses that pretended to care. The fake leader pays lip service to caring. These managers say they care, but there's no evidence of it in actual practice.

Nothing destroys credibility faster - robbing a manager of the respect needed to exercise authority - than to be insincere.

Such managers likely don't wake up in the morning and say to themselves: "I think that today, I'll be insincere and pretend that I give a damn." (or maybe some do).

It is typically the inability of the fake leader to manage themselves and their duties which creates the façade. Unable to free up the time it takes to care, but knowing that caring is important – they try to pull a fast one on the team.

Better to come right out and admit – "People, I'm swamped right now. Do you mind if you stay later so we can talk?"

Your team will understand. They'll give you some flack. But what they won't do is forgive you for trying to be someone you're not.

Therefore – be real.

Another toxin that hides in the boardroom is insecurity. You can identify an insecure boss in a second. He or she, rather than motivating their team, will attempt to compete with it. The insecure boss will also constantly ask the team for reassurance, as in "You think I'm right, don't you?"

It's not possible for an insecure person to be any kind of a real leader because their focus is not on the team. It's on themselves.

I believe we have many insecure people in management today because deep down, when they were promoted, they really didn't believe they had the "right stuff." As a result, they feel constantly threatened, not by anyone else, but by their own inner feeling of incompetence or inadequacy.

The insecure manager spends the day beating up on themselves.

If I have just described you, then you have some work to do.

Why do you think you were promoted in the first place? You must have value, at least in the eyes of those who gave you the position. If you don't think you deserve it, then in essence, you're also saying that the senior management group is made up of fools.

Recognize your own worth.

You must also shed the idea that you're a screw-up of the first order. Undertake small managerial tasks, the smaller the better at first. As you succeed at each task, you'll slowly gain confidence. Of course, you'll make mistakes – that's a given. But you can demonstrate to yourself that you're capable. You don't have to prove that to upper management or your team. They already assume it. Now, we just have to get you to believe it.

I'll know when you've finally succeeded in becoming a secure person, comfortable in your own skin, when you're brave enough to utter these 3 words: "I don't know."

Deep within our psyche is the inherent knowledge that – truth be known – we really don't have anything figured out. Not for certain anyway. We're all just winging it.

Few of us will ever admit that. And so, many of us pretend to know things that we don't. Rather than appear vulnerable, we try to display a shield of invincibility.

I knew a manager in the radio business, an industry riddled with insecurity, who responded to every single question with "Well, um - you see, it's like this..." You just knew he didn't have a clue what he was talking about.

It's better to admit that we don't know something, than to make things up on the fly, outright lie, or offer opinion without supporting facts. (There are management "gurus" who will tell you the opposite – that you should lie).

Your people don't expect you to be Yoda.

Be humble. And, after admitting you don't know something, always say you'll find out, because a major part of being real is learning. Your team will respect you more if you're not afraid to admit that, yes, they can show you a thing or two as well.

Finally, a word here about how we are physically coming across at work.

I want you to get rid of "serious face."

Stop frowning, squishing your face, putting on a scowl, gritting your teeth or doing anything else that makes you unpleasant to look at or be around.

Lighten up. Don't scare people.

As caring leaders, we are setting an example to be professional and human.

Inside, you may feel like an ogre and want to punch the world, but on the outside, you need to actually look like you care. Some will criticize me for this, saying that's faking it.

But in fact, if you smile and look contented – there's a good chance your sour mood will change and you'll become more receptive to the idea of giving a damn.

Do it for the team.

Food for thought: Project confidence and create a learning culture.

7 PAY ATTENTION TO WHAT YOUR PEOPLE WANT TO TALK ABOUT

**"The only reason why we ask other people how their weekend was is so we can tell them about our own weekend."
— Novelist Chuck Palahniuk**

When I was a manager, there was a time I was obsessed with making myself look good in the eyes of "upper management." Especially after first being promoted, my insecurities operated at a high level because the last thing I wanted was to screw up and get demoted, or worse yet, fired. As a result, I took my orders from the General Manager (GM).

What he cared about, I believed I also needed to care about. But as I'm about to point out, those were not the same things that my team cared about.

The GM, not surprisingly, was obsessed with reducing expenses and increasing profit. The way in which to do that, he believed, was to find ways to reduce the hours people worked, and if at all possible, get rid of the "deadwood" (his term for people I might have considered as poor performers).

Consideration for the feelings of our team never entered into any conversation I had with the GM. It simply was not on the radar.

The GM was always in a hurry. My meetings in his office, which I had hoped would be used to address my concerns, were instead, used by him to review the numbers. I accepted this, knowing he was a busy man. There wasn't time for him to mentor, coach or even encourage me. I was left to guess how I was doing as a manager.

As a new department head, I assumed that the GM's approach was what the company wanted all of its "leaders" to do.

And so, I would hold staff meetings in which I, just like my GM, would review the numbers. I talked also about the company's vision, it's competition and the challenges before us.

The staff seemed to appreciate these updates, but mostly - they had blank stares on their faces. I couldn't understand why they didn't seem to get excited about the company's plans.

Until one day, Jane - a new member of the team, entered my office and started to cry. She had moved from her hometown to work with us, but hadn't made any friends, including at the office. She asked me if we had any staff party's or social functions coming up where she could get to know some people, and not feel so lonely in a new town.

Here I was talking about spreadsheets, but Jane didn't care about those. The numbers had the power to impact her fate at the company, but for Jane, at that moment, finding a way out of her isolation was what really mattered to her. She needed me to be a human being. Not a boss.

What we as managers deal with every day - our responsibilities to the company, the reports we need to produce for our bosses, and the pressures we are under to meet the numbers - are, much to our dismay, not the preoccupations of our teams.

The team's concerns - social time with co-workers, taking additional training, how they're doing at work, how they're feeling - their hopes, dreams and challenges - are the topics of conversation that make the manager-to-worker connection more human.

The real leader understands that their purpose is not to befriend those they serve. But it's also not to become so distant that the team feels you're beyond approach.

Be casual in your interest of their lives. Ask how they're doing, what's new or how they feel today.

Say hello. (Shockingly, many readers of my "John" article reported that their managers refused to say hello, even when asked to do so).

Do not pry or meddle. Just be cool. Be a normal human being.

Food for thought: In offices the world over, there are plenty of to-do lists, task boards, schedules and orders that are top down. There are few genuine conversations.

8 THE FINE ART OF LISTENING

"Silence is one of the great arts of conversation."
- Greek Philosopher Cicero

Real leaders listen twice as much as they talk.

I believe there is an epidemic of over-communication in the workplace today from management and a colossal lack of listening. This has translated into a message to workers that what they have to say doesn't matter one bit.

Yet, listening is one of the most powerful tools in caring leadership. In fact, it's quite likely the most important method of acquiring respect and loyalty from your team. We all need to be heard.

Leadership expert Mark Murphy, CEO of "Leadership IQ" who teaches a course called "What Great Managers Do Differently" makes the point, in an article in Forbes magazine, that you know you're not being heard when your manager utters one of these phrases: "Life's not fair" and "You'll get over it."

For millions suffering from low self-esteem or anxiety, looking for support, these responses are not helpful.

I was fascinated to learn from research that when a manager talks to show his or her people how much they know; it actually hurts their credibility (and that's contrary to what we as managers generally believe). The research also found that "likeability" is reduced. Your people will find you to be unattractive as a leader, perhaps even repulsive, if you're constantly trying to prove that you're a know-it-all.

Another interesting fact we often overlook: your incessant talking is taking up time that is resulting in lost productivity by your team. And that's something upper management won't be happy about.

A survey from Harvard University (Social Cognitive and Affective Neuroscience Lab) discovered why our team will feel good if we just allow them to do the talking, as we sit back and listen. When a person is allowed to speak about themselves, it triggers the same chemical response (get ready for this) as when they're having sex. Dopamine is the neurotransmitter that is giving the brain a sense of pleasure.

One could argue that managers are depriving their people of dopamine. Rather than having team members who feel good about themselves, we're left with people who do not.

How then should we listen? There is a right way to do it - in a safe, caring environment, and a wrong way – to pursue hidden agendas.

It was the late great Stephen Covey (author of "The 7 Habits of Highly Effective People" and other bestsellers) who told us that we need to listen to understand, then speak to be understood.

But most of us aren't putting that into practice. We have decided that because life is too fast-paced, there is no time for listening, and besides, many of us feel, what others have to say is not as important as what we, as managers, have to say (an arrogant position if ever there was one).

Firstly, we absolutely need to maintain strong eye contact when we're listening to people. President John Kennedy, according to those who knew him well, could do this so that the person he was speaking to felt as though they were the most important person on earth.

He did this not by staring at someone non-stop, which can be viewed as creepy but instead, he allowed himself to close his eyes occasionally and move his head up and down to signal that he was taking it all in.

Have you ever spoken to someone, and rather than looking at you, they're checking their phone or reading something? They'll claim to be able to multi-task. But it's obvious, when it's their turn to speak, that they really did not listen.

The second practice is to keep your mind open. This is the part that I personally find difficult because when I'm speaking to a team member, I often have an agenda. I try to steer the conversation over to my way of thinking or to accomplish my goals.

We've all spoken to people who go further and are listening for the purpose of catching us making a mistake. Or they may be looking for proof that we don't know what we're talking about. Those are examples of hidden agendas as well.

Thirdly, in order to listen for understanding, we need to keep an ear out for these two things:

- How the person is feeling
- Why they feel the way they do

Feeling can be transmitted non-verbally. Take note if the person appears stressed, confused or troubled. Identifying how a person is feeling is one of the most effective ways to understand them.

The fourth technique, early in the conversation, is to confirm your understanding. Repeat back to the person your interpretation of what they said. "Have I got that right?"

If the answer is no, or at any time in the conversation, you're getting lost - ask follow-up questions. The best TV and radio interviewers will say "Can you tell me more about that?" if they feel they don't have the full story.

To summarize:

1. Make eye contact
2. Resist the urge to have an agenda and be totally open-minded
3. Listen for how the person feels and why
4. Confirm your understanding and follow up as needed

One thing to keep in mind. We can't really understand someone 100% unless we're familiar with their entire lives – their past history. That's because a person's view of the world is based not only on what they've learned, but what they've been through.

I don't know of any manager who believes they're a bad listener. We all think we've got this nailed when most of us don't. That's because the four powerful listening skills I have outlined are not easy. It takes practice.

We've been told that as managers, our job is to "tell people things."

The lack of time and the urgent need to get out our own messages has put an almost complete stop to real listening.

Yet - it is by listening, and only by listening, that we can get the big picture.

Food for thought: Are you just hearing, or are you really listening?

9 CREATING TOMORROW'S LEADERS

"I start with the premise that the function of leadership is to produce more leaders, not more followers." — Ralph Nader

A real leader doesn't hold people back. Instead, they empower, inspire and yes - push their teams to become the leaders of tomorrow.

We're going to need leaders that care in the future because of the incredible uncertainty before us. Caring will be the catalyst for the work which lies ahead to give humanity a chance to survive.

In a way, the real leader is a farmer - cultivating, planting seeds and watering - not crops, but people. In order for them to grow, be strong and take up the mantle.

I have divided this chapter into four actions you can take right now to start building the leaders of tomorrow.

1. Stand for Excellence

One of the mistakes that can be made is to assume caring leadership is passive. That all we have to do is sit back and let people do as they choose.

Nothing could be farther from the truth.

The caring leader stands for excellence and demands - yes, that is the word we must use - DEMANDS - excellence from everyone on the team. If you care about someone, you want them to be extremely good at what they do. You want them to aim for the stars and be at the top of their game.

Your job is give the team all of the tools, resources, information, encouragement, guidance, and support that they need to be excellent at what they do.

That means you have to strive for excellence too.

2. Demand People respect each other

The deterioration of common courtesy in the business world has always bothered me to an extreme. Somewhere along the line it became acceptable to ignore people and be rude.

The University of California conducted research and found that the degree to which people are happy is related to how much respect they receive from others.

We don't feel respected when our pleas for help are pushed aside, when our concerns are trivialized, and when we're not being heard.

There's the issue of respect or lack thereof between manager and worker, but there's also the issue of whether team members respect each other.

That's just as important.

Instill within your team that mutual respect is a necessary component of teamwork and the key to achieving organizational objectives.

3. Tell people what they need to hear

As real leaders, we're not doing anybody a favor by telling them what they want to hear, rather than what they need to hear.

People need to know where they stand and most importantly, what they're good at.

They're not always the best judge of their own strengths and weaknesses. It often takes a seasoned outside observer to identify talent.

Similarly, we have an obligation to tell people when they're putting their reputations at risk.

For example, I have numerous people who have failed to get back to clients in a timely fashion. In today's competitive environment, I believe that acknowledging communications as quick as possible is a must. (You snooze you lose). If I don't have time to respond to someone in detail, I always at least let them know that I received their email, text or voicemail and I tell them when I'll be getting back to them.

I believe if you don't communicate within a reasonable length of time, people will assume you're not interested. That may not be the actual case, but it's the conclusion that is reached.

A person's reputation can be damaged if they don't reply, especially to very important clients.

Rather than letting it go, I make sure that anyone who works with me is aware of my policy on communications.

If you care about your people - their reputation, and by association - your own reputation and that of your entire organization - you won't hold back on telling them what they need to know.

4. Be loyal to the work

This one may surprise you. But I feel it's important to ask your team to be loyal, not to you personally and not even to the organization, but to the work.

It's the quality of the work that will determine if someone has a future in their chosen field or not.

If we care, as managers, then we'll put the emphasis on where it belongs - and that's not on you. It's the work your people are doing.

When we tell people to be loyal to the work, they receive a message loud and clear - that yes, the boss really does care about whether I'm good at what I do.

It's important for me to stress the fact that the reputation your people have is going to affect your reputation as the manager. It will also affect how people see the entire organization.

A real leader knows that we're all in this together.

To summarize:

1. Stand for excellence
2. Demand people respect each other
3. Tell people what they need to hear
4. Ask the team to be loyal to the work, not to you

Beyond these four pillars, get the heck out of the way and be a cheerleader. Jump in when you see something wonderful going on, to say "You nailed it!" If you see things that aren't so wonderful, resist telling people "how it's done." Instead, explain how *you* would do it. Finally, remember the great words of Benjamin Franklin: "Tell me and I forget, teach me and I may remember, involve me and I learn."

Food for thought: A real leader demands people aim for excellence and mutual respect, so they can become real leaders too.

10 PUTTING THE MEANING BACK INTO WORK

"Better to sleep all day on a park bench than do work you don't believe in."
— Author Marty Rubin

Today, people want their work and lives to have meaning.

We're tired of just chasing the almighty dollar, leaving us with a feeling of emptiness. Young people in particular, would rather take a pay cut to do a job that's making a difference in the world.

Psychologists tell us that the rise of depression and suicide can be linked, in part, to a general sense of meaninglessness. Many occupations and tasks don't appear to contribute to any greater cause. We seem to be "feeding the wheel" - pushing a machine that's generating money for corporate entities, for what purpose, we don't really know.

As I write these words, there are people everywhere thinking of leaving their jobs because the emptiness is making them unhappy, perhaps even sick.

In the days when I owned a graphic design firm, my best designers would produce incredible ads, posters and newsletter covers that we presented to clients for consideration. But much to the horror of my team, some clients, rather than reviewing the work and giving us feedback, would simply not bother to look at it.

This had irritated one designer who came to me and said "What's the point of any of this? The work means nothing to these people. We end up discarding it. I am paid well, but I don't feel fulfilled."

Real leaders understand this frustration and do something about it.

I've produced this list of six key areas that can be pursued.

1. Show how tasks connect to the ultimate outcome

Draw a line between what people are doing and the ultimate benefit of the resulting product, service or deliverable, listing all the steps in-between. A visual of the path between departments leading up to a positive outcome will give your team a renewed sense of accomplishment. For example, as a worker, I might be producing a spreadsheet on air flow, passed to an analyst who in turn, uses the data to help homebuilders construct houses that use less energy. Each task, no matter how menial it may seem, becomes important when we understand how it's connected in the chain of development.

2. Let team members experience the end result of their work

It helps if people can experience the benefit of the end product. Using my example above, the spreadsheet worker would walk into the environmentally friendly home resulting from the data they produced.

3. Provide opportunities to be challenged and to learn

More meaningful work results when people are challenged. Ask the team to come up with better methods, higher standards of quality or ways to achieve greater efficiency. Also look at having team members switch jobs so they are constantly learning. This has the added benefit of everyone on the team fully understanding everyone else's job.

4. Provide opportunities for veterans to teach newcomers

People will enjoy more meaning in their work when they have the chance to share their knowledge and experience. Allow experienced team members to mentor, teach and guide others.

5. Give control over the work environment

One of the biggest complaints of workers is the lack of control over their own work environment. Let go of micro-managing so people have the time to think, make their own decisions, and set up the systems and techniques that work best for them. If flex-hours and working from home make sense, allow it to happen.

6. Move people into areas that match their values

People want to be involved in work that's important to them. Find out what their values are and see if you can match those interests with other opportunities in the organization. For example, if they want to help other workers, is there a way to move them from an isolated computer job to putting on workshops?

Finding out what's really important to your people is key to developing a strategy that gives them meaning. But there will be cases where it just doesn't work out. Their values, and the work being done, may not be compatible.

It's in those cases when the real leader helps his or her people come up with a plan to secure the meaning they seek, even if it ultimately results in their leaving the organization.

Food for thought: Have you done your best to make the work meaningful?

11 EVEN AFTER THEY LEAVE

"Encourage, lift and strengthen one another. For the positive energy spread to one will be felt by us all. For we are connected, one and all."
— Mental health expert Deborah Day

One of the things that most resonated with people about my article on John, the Caring leader, was his support for team members even after they left the company.

In fact, some have argued that being a lifetime coach is perhaps the distinguishing factor in real leadership - because it's the one thing that proves the leader really did care about the person after all.

We live in a throw-away society where everything seems easily dispensable, including the people in our lives. Our Facebook friends are primarily people we don't know and will never meet. Real face-to-face friendship is increasingly rare. A study by Cornell University says most people now have only two close friends, down from three friends 25 years ago.

Real leaders will be there for us - for advice and support - years after we're no longer working with them.

That's rare because in the minds of many managers, a departing employee is someone to be forgotten, no longer under influence, or dare I say it - no longer "owned."

There is of course no obligation whatsoever to stay in touch with people. And that's the beauty of it. Real leaders do it just because they care.

The nature of the relationship does change - from "boss" to strictly "mentor" - and yes, perhaps even "friend." Once an employee has left the organization, friendship can enter the picture and there is nothing wrong with that.

I've never had the good fortune of a former boss staying in my life - not even John. As the years pass, the possibilities diminish more and more.

But it is our memory of real leaders that can linger. We remember their kindness, thoughtfulness and sincere desire to help us be the best that we can be.

That can apply, regardless of the circumstances of departure.

John was that special kind of leader who could fire you and you still thought he was the greatest thing since sliced bread. He never fired people for the wrong reasons. It wasn't because he disliked you.

I'm old enough to remember when, in 1978, the Chairman of Ford Motor Company, Henry Ford II (who was the eldest son of the original Henry Ford of Model T fame) fired his President, the late great Lee Iacocca. Lee recalled that fateful day when Henry called him into the office and explained the firing this way: "Sometimes you just don't like somebody."

A dismissal from John was always because he didn't feel your skills matched the position you were in. A believer in "building on strength" John tried to put you into a job that allowed your talents to shine, but if no such job existed, he would encourage you to find one on the outside that did - and here's the kicker - he would often help you do it.

People dread that meeting in which they're told it's over. John had a way of making you realize he was doing you a favor. Of course, you refused to believe it during the moment you were sacked. But most people, afterwards, would thank John and tell him he was right.

You may say to me that is not realistic in today's world. There just isn't any time to help people. We're all on our own.

But the truth is, we'll make time for whatever is important to us. If helping people is important to you, then you'll make the time for it. Somehow. Some way.

I've always loved this quote from the ancient Chinese philosopher Lao Tzu: Time is a created thing. To say 'I don't have time,' is like saying, 'I don't want to.' It's the truth.

I think the important thing about this chapter is the significance of supporting people after they've left us - the impact that has on society as a whole. A real leader looks at the big picture - her or his role in the larger scheme of things. They see themselves as not just running a team, department or organization - but as someone who is nurturing the development of people for the betterment of their industry, their e community and society as a whole.

As a manager, you're influence can extend well beyond the walls of your office. It can extend into the lives of people decades after you've worked with them.

Food for thought: Do you care enough to check on people even after they've left?

12 BEING A REAL LEADER CAN BE RISKY, BUT IT SHOULDN'T BE

"Life is either a daring adventure or nothing at all."
— Helen Keller

I wasn't sure about this chapter, but let's face it. Not every organization will support you if you decide to act in the best interest of your people.

When I first became a manager at the age of 27, I was, by far, the worst manager ever to set foot in an office. I believed, as do some managers today, that I "owned" my people. As a result, I felt I was free to mistreat them.

It wasn't long before another manager took me aside and explained that I could get much better results if I treated the team with respect and dignity.

Eventually, inspired by one of my immediate supervisors, the caring John, I did just that. And I went all out.

But then, a memorable day arrived.

It was the day when the big cheese called me into his office and got right to the point, saying: "You need to fire everybody." Silence. I then asked, "Everybody?" His answer: "Yes, we don't need all those people around here. But we'll keep you." I asked what would happen if I refused to fire all 16 hard-working souls, and of course, you know what the answer to that was. I would be fired. And he - the Grand Poobah - would personally do the dirty deed.

I chose to resign, but before I did, I called my team into a meeting and let them know they'd all be out on the street in a few days. The least I could do, I felt, was to give them as much warning as possible.

At the highest levels of the corporate ladder, there may not be a lot of sympathy for you as a caring manager. In view of all the evidence I have presented in this book, there most certainly should be.

Caring, as we've learned, is good for business. But what "should be" is not always "what is" on this crazy planet of ours.

When push comes to shove, as it did for me, we are forced to make a decision. Do we hold true to our commitment to protect our team, to have their backs, and defend them at every turn? Or do we throw them under the bus and save our own skin?

The lesson I learned during that horrible time, and the message I need to relay to you now - is that it comes down to character. What kind of a person are you? Really? My team never blamed me for what happened. They did appreciate my warning as to what was about to take place.

I know one thing. Had I decided to stay on and fire the team, there was a 99 per cent chance that eventually, I would be let go too.

Years later, I heard from some of the team members, eager to update me on their progress in life and to learn whatever became of me.

I chose to leave the corporate world entirely and set up my own shop. I told the people I hired that I never wanted to be called a "boss" or even a "leader". Rather, I was the "support person" - the guy who makes sure everyone has the tools, resources and backing to get the job done.

The credit for whatever we've accomplished as a company has gone entirely to the great people who work with me. And notice I said "with" not "for". Because if we're truly a team, there isn't any "for" about it.

Some members of the team have been with me for 12 years, but in that whole time, they have grown immensely. It's been a pleasure to witness.

Caring leadership, the kind I've talked about in this book, isn't confined to the walls of a boardroom. It's not a gimmick to trick people into working harder. And it's certainly not a badge you can wear to make yourself feel good or important.

It's really just about being a decent human being.

And so, if you're stuck in an environment where caring is looked down upon and people are not viewed as human, maybe - just maybe – it's not the place for you.

Food for thought: Do you work for a caring organization?

EPILOGUE: IN DEFENSE OF MANAGERS

When I asked people for feedback on this book, I was told caring is a two-way street. Managers wanted me to know that they too need some tender loving care and that abuse from workers was common.

My response was that the ability to reverse that lies with them. It has to start from the top. I firmly believe that if the leader becomes more human, so too will the team.

Of course, not every manager will care as much as their team needs. Not every worker will care as much as the leader needs.

And in defense of managers everywhere, it's not an easy road. Today's tight budgets, impossible deadlines and demands by shareholders all make being a manager one of the most difficult jobs on the planet.

If you're running a team of any kind, you have my utmost respect. I've been there, and I'm still there. I know it's not easy. And much of what I preach in this book, I am still learning to implement myself.

By and large, we managers are not bad people. To the contrary, most of us want to do a good job. Most want to be respected. Most would rather help people than hurt them.

But somehow, in the last few decades, we've become a society that has lost its way. I have referred often in this book to what I call the culture of neglect. We can debate until the cows come home as to why that has been allowed to happen. Whether it's today's preoccupation with profit, with "self" or with a technological revolution that has put speed above quiet contemplation - one thing is certain.

Today's manager has a huge responsibility to help turn the tide. The challenge is to find the time and perhaps more importantly - the space within our hearts - to give a damn.

God's speed.

ABOUT THE AUTHOR

Cory Galbraith is a business owner, writer and researcher who resides in Ontario, Canada. He is passionate about helping people find their purpose, be the best they can be, and see life as an adventure, not the struggle we often allow it to be.

www.ingramcontent.com/pod-product-compliance
Lightning Source LLC
Chambersburg PA
CBHW030736180526
45157CB00008BA/3198